HOW MACHINES WORK

MOTORBIKES

CHRIS OXLADE

W
FRANKLIN WATTS
LONDON•SYDNEY

An Appleseed Editions book

First published in 2008 by Franklin Watts

Franklin Watts
338 Euston Road, London NW1 3BH

Franklin Watts Australia
Level 17/207 Kent St, Sydney, NSW 2000

© 2008 Appleseed Editions

Appleseed Editions Ltd
Well House, Friars Hill, Guestling, East Sussex TN35 4ET

Created by Q2AMedia
Series Editor: Honor Head
Book Editor: Harriet McGregor
Senior Art Director: Ashita Murgai
Designers: Harleen Mehta, Ravijot Singh
Picture Researcher: Amit Tigga

ISBN 978 0 7496 8075 6

Dewey classification: 629.227' 5
All words in **bold** can be found in Glossary on pages 30–31.

Website information is correct at time of going to press. However, the publishers cannot
accept liability for any information or links found on third-party websites.

A CIP catalogue for this book is available from the British Library.

Picture credits
t=top b=bottom c=centre l=left r=right m=middle
Cover Images: Main image: ©BMW AG

American Honda Motor Co., Inc.: 4, 5t, 5b, BMW AG: 6, Nick Stubbs: 7t, Amy Walters/ Shutterstock: 7b,
Triumph Motorcycles: 8tr, BMW AG: 8ml, Baloncici/ Shutterstock: 8br, American Honda Motor Co., Inc.: 9t, 9b,
Michael G. Mill/ Shutterstock: 10 inset, BMW AG: 10b, American Honda Motor Co. Inc.: 11t, 13t,
Baloncici/ Shutterstock: 13b, BMW AG:14, Martin Prihoda/ Istockphoto: 15t, Phill Clarke: 15b,
American Honda Motor Co. Inc.: 16, 17t, 17b, 18, BMW AG: 19t, American Honda Motor Co., Inc.: 19b,
Chua Kah Chun/ Shutterstock: 20t, Stephen McSweeny/ Shutterstock: 20b, American Honda Motor Co., Inc.: 21t,
Ioannis Ioannou/ Shutterstock: 21b, Ducati Motor Holding S.p.A.: 22, American Honda Motor Co., Inc.: 23t,
Confederate Motorcycles: 23b, Kawasaki Racing Team: 24, Frank Kletschkus/ Alamy: 25t, Pasphotography/ Shutterstock: 25b,
Fred Goldstein/ Shutterstock: 26, Intelligent Energy: 27 inset, 27b, Dodge: 28, rMOTO: 29

Q2AMedia Art Bank: 11, 12

Printed in Hong Kong

Franklin Watts is a division of Hachette Children's Books

CONTENTS

MOTORBIKES

Modern motorbikes are extremely high-tech machines. Their powerful engines give them amazing acceleration and terrifying top speeds.

MOTORBIKE TYPES

All motorbikes have a **frame**, two wheels and an engine. Street bikes are good for general use, such as getting round town. Cruisers are designed to make their riders look cool! Giant **tourers** are for long journeys and camping trips. Sports road bikes and racing superbikes are for thrills. Off-road bikes are for racing on dirt tracks and for doing jumps and tricks.

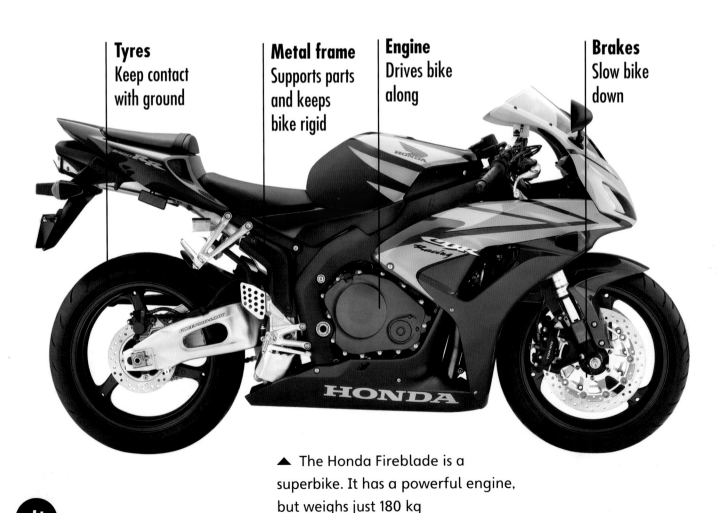

Tyres
Keep contact with ground

Metal frame
Supports parts and keeps bike rigid

Engine
Drives bike along

Brakes
Slow bike down

▲ The Honda Fireblade is a superbike. It has a powerful engine, but weighs just 180 kg

◀ Racing bikes are as powerful and as light as possible. A rider needs great skill to ride one quickly

▼ Off-road bikes have special features, such as chunky tyres and high suspension, for travelling over rough ground

DID YOU KNOW?
Some of the first motorbikes were powered by small steam engines

Long front suspension

Skid plate to protect engine

High clearance under body

MOTORBIKE ENGINES

In most motorbikes, the engine is at the bottom of the frame. Big motorbikes have engines with the same power as those in small cars.

ENGINE CYLINDERS

Motorbike engines come in different shapes and sizes, but all of them have similar parts. Inside all engines are one or more can-shaped **cylinders**. **Pistons** fit snugly inside the cylinders, and slide up and down. The pistons are connected to the **crankshaft**.

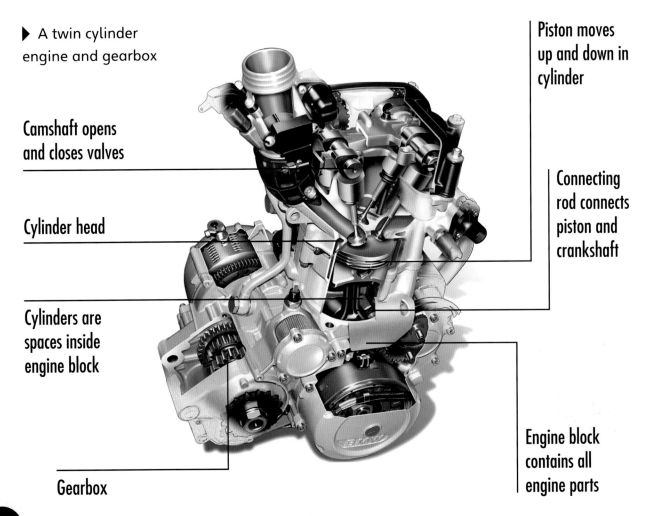

▶ A twin cylinder engine and gearbox

Camshaft opens and closes valves

Cylinder head

Cylinders are spaces inside engine block

Gearbox

Piston moves up and down in cylinder

Connecting rod connects piston and crankshaft

Engine block contains all engine parts

Fuel tank

VALVES

Valves open and let a mixture of fuel and air into the cylinders. Valves also let waste gases out of the cylinders. The valves are opened and closed by a **camshaft**. Waste gases go along the **exhaust** pipes and escape into air.

▶ Fuel for the engine goes along a pipe from the fuel tank to the engine

DID YOU KNOW?
Motorcycle engines work at very high speeds. In a typical sports bike engine, the pistons move up and down more than 100 times each second

Exhaust pipes

▶ The exhaust system takes waste gases away from the engine and into the air at the back of the bike

ENGINE LAYOUTS

Motorbike engines come in a variety of shapes and sizes. A **single-cylinder** engine has one cylinder. A **twin** engine has two cylinders. These can be arranged in three different ways:

1) Side by side (a parallel twin)

2) Opposite each other (an opposed twin or boxer)

3) At an angle to each other (a V-twin)

Many larger bikes have four cylinders arranged in a straight line (a straight four). The capacity is the total space inside the cylinders. A single cylinder can range from 50 cc to more than 1000 cc. One cc is one cubic centimetre.

▼ Some large BMW bikes have an opposed twin engine (also known as a boxer). The cylinders stick out on each side of the bike, next to the rider's feet

▲ This is an 865 cc parallel twin engine

▶ The V-twin is a classic engine layout found on many American motorbikes

MEGA ENGINES

Big touring machines have plenty of luxury equipment, and often carry two people and luggage. This adds up to a lot of weight. These motorbikes need big, powerful engines for good acceleration and smooth running on long journeys. The biggest tourers have six-cylinder, 1800 cc engines – bigger than the engines in family cars. The American Boss Hoss has a 5700 cc engine!

▼ The famous Honda Gold Wing tourer, with its bodywork removed. It is powered by an opposed six-cylinder engine

Metal frame
Supports parts and keeps bike rigid

HONDA GOLD WING	
Specification	
Engine:	opposed six-cylinder, 1832 cc
Power:	117 horsepower/87 kW
Weight	363 kg (800 lb)
Length:	2.64 m (8.66 ft)

Large exhaust

DID YOU KNOW?
A large single-cylinder engine is known as a 'thumper' because it makes a thump–thump noise as it works

Three cylinders on each side of engine

HOW ENGINES WORK

The push that an engine gives to a motorbike's wheels comes from small explosions in its cylinders. Most motorbikes have four-stroke engines.

THE FOUR-STROKE CYCLE

Each movement of a piston in or out of its cylinder is known as a stroke. In a four-stroke engine, a piston goes through a sequence of **four strokes** again and again. This sequence is called the four-stroke cycle.

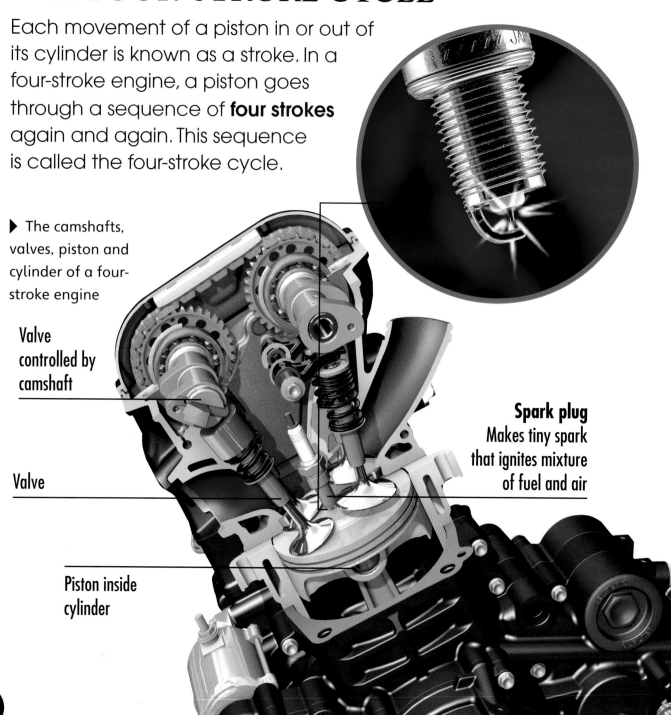

▶ The camshafts, valves, piston and cylinder of a four-stroke engine

Valve controlled by camshaft

Valve

Piston inside cylinder

Spark plug
Makes tiny spark that ignites mixture of fuel and air

Camshaft

▲ A camshaft spins once per cycle. Egg-shaped pieces of metal along it force the inlet and outlet valves open

WHAT HAPPENS

During the cycle, a camshaft opens and closes the valves at the top of the cylinder to let in fuel and let out waste gases. In an engine with two or more cylinders, the different strokes happen at different times in each cylinder, which makes the engine run smoothly.

THE FOUR-STROKE CYCLE

① INLET STROKE

The piston moves down, sucking a mixture of fuel and air into the cylinder.

Cylinder   Piston

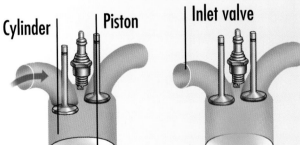

▲ Inlet valve open

② COMPRESSION STROKE

The piston moves up, squeezing the mixture into the top of the cylinder.

Inlet valve

▲ Valves closed

③ POWER STROKE

The spark plug ignites the mixture. The explosion pushes the piston down.

Spark plug Ignites fuel

▲ Valves closed

④ EXHAUST STROKE

The piston moves up, pushing the waste gases from the explosion out of the cylinder.

Outlet valve

▲ Outlet valve open

TWO-STROKE ENGINES

Some motorbikes have **two-stroke** engines instead of four-stroke engines. Two-stroke engines are simpler and lighter than four-stroke engines of the same size. They don't need a camshaft or valves. They produce more power but give out more pollution than four-strokes. This is because the exhaust contains oil and unburned fuel.

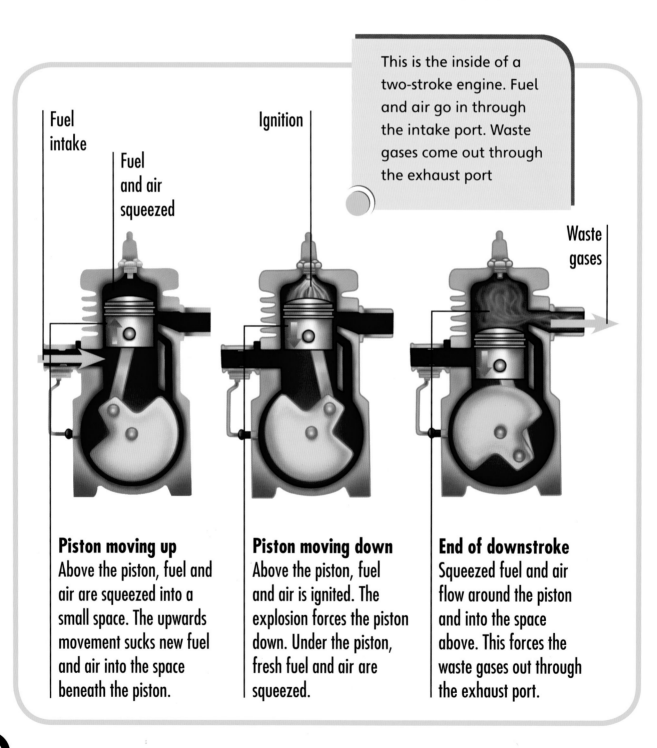

Fuel intake

Fuel and air squeezed

Ignition

This is the inside of a two-stroke engine. Fuel and air go in through the intake port. Waste gases come out through the exhaust port

Waste gases

Piston moving up
Above the piston, fuel and air are squeezed into a small space. The upwards movement sucks new fuel and air into the space beneath the piston.

Piston moving down
Above the piston, fuel and air is ignited. The explosion forces the piston down. Under the piston, fresh fuel and air are squeezed.

End of downstroke
Squeezed fuel and air flow around the piston and into the space above. This forces the waste gases out through the exhaust port.

Two-stroke engines are often used on off-road bikes because they are light and powerful

COOLING

When the fuel explodes and burns in an engine's cylinders, it produces a lot of heat. Friction between the moving parts also produces heat. The engine must be cooled, otherwise the parts become extremely hot and the engine seizes up. Motorbike engines are cooled either by water flowing through the engine block (water cooling) or by air flowing around the outside of the cylinders (air cooling).

These fins are on an air-cooled engine. When the bike is moving, air flows over them and cools the engine

13

TRANSMISSION

A motorbike's transmission is made up of the parts that connect the engine to the rear wheel. On most motorbikes these parts are the clutch, gearbox and chain.

THE GEAR BOX

A motorbike's gears let the engine turn the rear wheel at different speeds. A rider uses low gears for slow speeds and high gears for fast speeds. The engine turns one set of **cogs** in the **gear box**. These cogs turn another set of cogs, which drive the rear wheel.

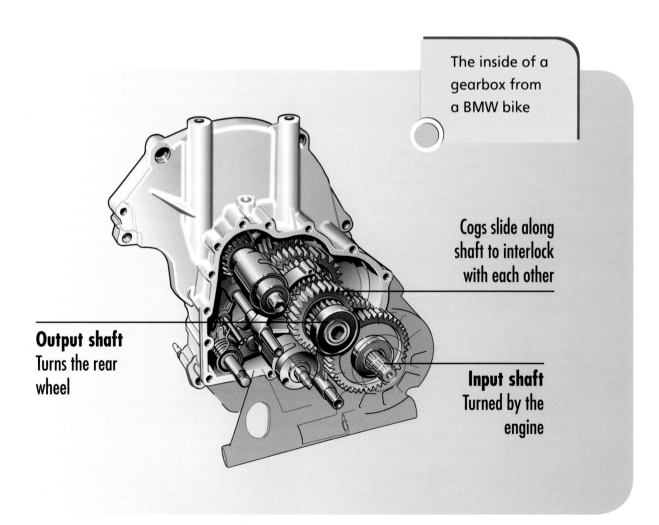

The inside of a gearbox from a BMW bike

Cogs slide along shaft to interlock with each other

Output shaft
Turns the rear wheel

Input shaft
Turned by the engine

CHANGING GEAR

To change speed, the rider must change gear. Before the rider changes gear, the engine must be disconnected from the gearbox. The clutch disconnects the engine from the gearbox. The rider can then change gear. Large bikes have five or six gears.

▶ The rider changes gear by pressing down or lifting up the gear-change lever with the left foot

DID YOU KNOW?
Motorbikes have no reverse gear, but some heavy touring bikes have an electric motor for reversing

▼ A motorcycle clutch is made up of two sets of plates. When the plates press against each other, the engine turns the rear wheel

CHAIN DRIVES

Most motorbikes have a chain drive. This means the rear wheel is turned by a loop of chain from the gear box. The chain goes around two wheels that have teeth around their rims. These are called sprocket wheels.

The front sprocket wheel is turned by the output shaft of the gear box. The rear sprocket wheel is in the centre of the rear wheel of the motorbike. The front sprocket wheel pulls on the chain, and the chain pulls on the rear sprocket wheel.

Chain

Sprocket wheel on back wheel

The chain must be kept just at the right tightness otherwise it vibrates up and down as it moves

BELT OR SHAFT

A few motorbikes do not have chain drives. Instead, they have belt drives or shaft drives. A belt drive is similar to a chain drive, except that power is transferred from the gear box to the wheels by a wide belt. In a shaft drive, the rear wheel is turned by a spinning shaft (rod) from the gearbox. Shaft drives are quieter than chain drives.

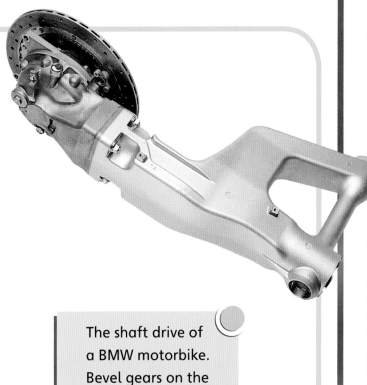

The shaft drive of a BMW motorbike. Bevel gears on the end of the shaft turn the wheel

▼ An all-terrain vehicle (ATV) is like a motorbike on four wheels. Some ATVs have all-wheel drive

HONDA TRX420TM

Specification

Engine:	single-cylinder, 420 cc
Drive:	shaft drive to rear wheels
Weight:	237 kg (522 lb)
Length:	2.05 m (6.74 ft)

ALL ABOUT WHEELS

Tyres must grip the road to let the bike accelerate, brake and turn corners. The suspension keeps the tyres on the road as the bike goes over bumps.

SUSPENSION

A motorbike's **suspension** lets the wheels move up and down as they go over bumps. **Suspension units** have springs to let the wheel rise and fall. They also have devices called **dampers** which stop the bike bouncing up and down repeatedly on the springs after going over a bump.

Swing arm suspension on the back wheel

Damper
Stops bike bouncing up and down too much

Swing arm

TYPES OF SUSPENSION

Modern motorbikes normally have a telescopic **fork** suspension on the front wheel and a **swing arm** suspension on the rear wheel.

Off-road bikes have long suspension units that can absorb big bumps and heavy landings

Fork

▲ The long-travel suspension of an off-road bike is designed to soak up the bumps on rough ground

HONDA CRF450R

Specification

Engine:	single cylinder, 449 cc
Power:	51 horsepower/38 kW
Drive:	chain
Weight:	103 kg (227 lb)
Length:	2.19 m (7.18 ft)

◀ Motorbike tyres have a rounded cross-section. This allows them to keep gripping the road when a rider leans a bike on a bend. These racing bikes have smooth (slick) tyres

WHEELS

A motorbike's wheels turn to let the bike move along the road. The rear wheel also pushes the motorbike along.

A wheel is made up of a hub and a rim. The hub lets the wheel turn easily. The rim supports the tyre and keeps it in shape. Between the hub and the rim are spokes.

▶ Road motorbike tyres have grooves that squeeze out water so that the tyre can grip on wet roads. This is the wide wheel of a custom bike

BRAKES

Brakes slow a motorbike down. There are brakes on both the front and the rear wheels. They are both a type of brake called a disc brake. Attached to each wheel is a metal disc. Brake pads squeeze the discs, which slows the wheels. The brakes are operated by using the right foot pedal and the right-hand lever on the handlebar.

Brake disc attached to wheel

Brake pads

A cutaway image of a motorbike's brake disc and brake pads

This cylinder presses the brake pads onto the disc

▼ The disc brake of a sports bike. The holes in the wheel lets the disc cool after heavy braking

Brake calliper
Contains brake pads

Brake disc
Attached to wheel

DID YOU KNOW?
Slick tyres are smooth, with no tread at all. They are used on race tracks, but only in dry weather

STRUCTURE AND DESIGN

A motorbike has a strong, metal frame that holds all the other parts in position. A strong, rigid frame is important for good handling at high speeds.

TUBULAR AND LATTICE FRAMES

There are several different types of motorbike frame. Many motorbikes still use a traditional tubular frame, which is made up of metal tubes welded together, similar to the frame of a bicycle. A lattice frame is made up of two frames on either side of the motorbike.

The Ducati Monster 696 model has a lattice frame (painted red here)

Headstock holds front forks in place

Engine hangs under frame

Lattice frame made from metal tubes

▼ The Honda CBR 600RR
has an aluminium perimeter
frame that supports its
powerful 599 cc engine

HONDA CBR 600RR

Specification

Engine:	in-line four cylinder, 599 cc
Power:	115 horsepower/86 kW
Drive:	chain
Weight:	163 kg (359 lb)
Length:	2.01 m (6.59 ft)

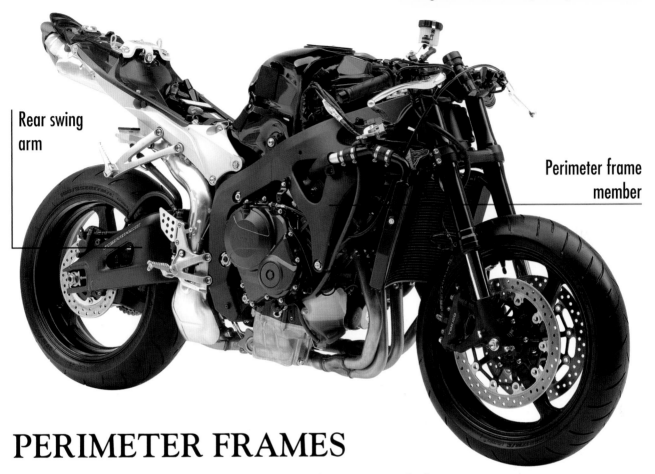

Rear swing
arm

Perimeter frame
member

PERIMETER FRAMES

A perimeter frame is made up of thick metal
bars that bend around the outside of the
engine. The frame has mounting points for the
other parts, such as the engine and suspension.

◀ On the Confederate
Hellcat the engine block
is actually part of the
frame. It is known as a
structural member

SHAPED FOR SPEED

Faster bikes, such as sport bikes and superbikes, are fitted with lightweight bodywork called fairings. This gives the motorbike a smooth shape. It lets the bike cut through the air more easily than a bike without bodywork. It reduces a pull called **drag** that is made by the air as the bike moves forwards. The front fairing includes a low windscreen for the driver to look through.

This race rider is ducking down behind the front fairing to reduce drag as much as possible

Side fairings
With engine
air intakes

Front fairing
and windscreen

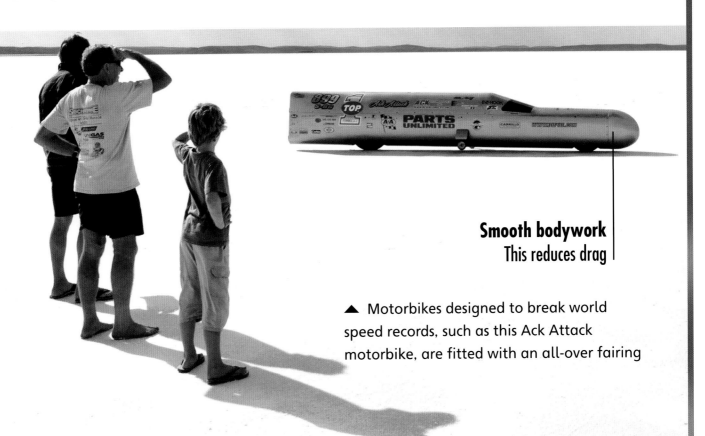

Smooth bodywork
This reduces drag

▲ Motorbikes designed to break world
speed records, such as this Ack Attack
motorbike, are fitted with an all-over fairing

INSIDES OUT

Some motorbikes have no bodywork at all. These are not
bikes designed for racing or touring, but for showing off on
the streets! They are designed so that you can see all the
machinery that works the bike. They have large engines
that make a loud roar. Custom bikes have many parts
removed by their owners so that all the machinery is visible.

▶ The design of this bike is
called a chopper

Long forks

**Stylised
bodywork**

Low seat

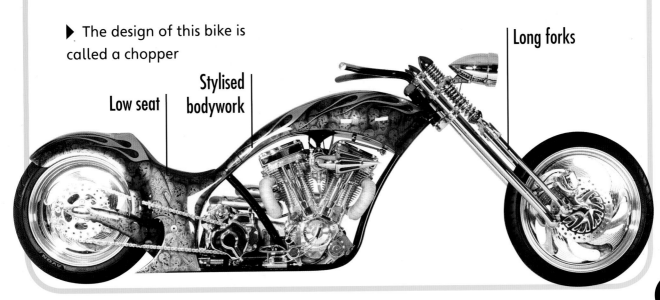

NEW AND FUTURE BIKES

Modern motorbikes have complex electronics that make them fast, efficient and safe. Many features come from technology designed for racing bikes.

ELECTRIC MOTORBIKES

Electric motorbikes are beginning to appear on the streets. These bikes are not as powerful or fast as bikes with petrol engines. However, they are quiet and very efficient – perfect for riding around towns and cities. On existing electric motorbikes, the electricity comes from a battery.

An electric scooter is powered by an electric motor attached to the rear wheel

FUEL CELL MOTORBIKES

New electric motorbikes that are powered by fuel cells are also being produced. Fuel cells make electricity from fuels such as hydrogen and methanol. They are like batteries that can be recharged by adding more fuel. The only waste from a hydrogen fuel cell is water.

This is the fuel cell from an Emissions Neutral Vehicle (ENV) bike

▼ This is the ENV motorbike. It is powered by a hydrogen fuel cell. These bikes are being trialled around the world, but are not yet available to buy

Drive belt from electric motor

CONCEPT BIKES

Motorbike designers often design bikes to show what they think future motorbikes might look like. These bikes are called concept bikes. They feature incredible new ideas and technology. All of them look amazing. Some look weird. Designers show off their concept bike ideas to the public at motorbike shows. Most concept bikes never get produced for people to buy.

This incredible machine is the Dodge Tomahawk concept bike. It features an 8.3 litre engine from a Dodge Viper sports car

This is the Robrady rMOTO Electric Superbike concept. It is almost silent but performs like a superbike!

◀ The electric motor drives the rear wheel, and the batteries are recharged as the bike brakes and slows down

THREE-WHEELED CONCEPTS

Although you probably think of motorbikes as two-wheeled machines, a few designs have three wheels. They are known as trikes. They are useful for carrying passengers, touring and cruising. They normally have two wheels at the rear, so they don't fall over when the rider stops. Designers have devised some concept three-wheelers that look nothing like any motorcycle you've seen before!

GLOSSARY

Camshaft Shaft in an engine that opens and closes the cylinder's valves as it spins

cc Short for cubic centimetre. Engine capacity is normally measured in cc or in cubic inches

Cog Wheel with teeth around its edge

Crankshaft Shaft that is turned by the pistons in an engine

Cylinder Can-shaped space inside an engine where fuel burns

Damper Part of a suspension unit that stops a wheel bouncing up and down after a bump. Also called a shock absorber

Drag The pull that air exerts on a motorcycle as it moves forwards. It tries to slow the motorbike

Exhaust Parts of a motorbike that carry waste gases away from the engine

Forks Two suspension units that support a motorbike's front wheel

Four-stroke Engine that produces power on every other downstroke of a piston

Frame Part of a motorbike that keeps the bike rigid and supports all its other parts. Also called a chassis

Gear box Part of the transmission. It allows the engine to turn the wheels at different speeds

Piston Part of an engine that slides up and down in a cylinder

Single-cylinder Engine with just one cylinder and piston

Suspension Part of a motorbike that lets the wheels move up and down as the motorbike goes over bumps, keeping the tyres in contact with the road

Suspension unit Part of a motorbike suspension, made up of a spring and a damper

Swing arm Part of a motorbike that connects the rear wheel to the frame. It lets the rear wheel move up and down

Tourer Large motorbike used for travelling long distances

Transmission Parts of a motorbike that transfer movement from the engine to the wheels

Twin Engine with two cylinders and pistons

Two-stroke Engine that produces power on every downstroke of a piston

Valve Part of an engine that opens to let fuel into a cylinder (an inlet valve) or to let exhaust gases out (an exhaust valve)

INDEX

Websites

www.discoverychannel.co.uk/motorbikes/index.shtml
Motorbike history and motorbike racing

http://auto.howstuffworks.com/motorcycle.htm
Find out how motorbikes work

http://www.keveney.com/twostroke.html
See an animation of the two-stroke engine cycle